Contents

Who was Shakespeare?

Shakespeare the actor   4

Shakespeare's plays   6

Who was Nelson?   7

In the Navy   8

Nelson the hero   10

Who was Queen Victoria?   12

Victoria becomes Queen   14

Diamond Jubilee   15

The British Empire   16

The Battle of Trafalgar

Who was Shakespeare?

This is Asa. He lives in Shakespeare Road.

His road is named after a writer called William Shakespeare, who lived 400 years ago.

Shakespeare wrote plays and poems. He is even more famous today than he was in his own lifetime. This is what Asa found out about him.

Shakespeare was born in a town called Stratford-upon-Avon. If you go there you can see the house where he was born.

Shakespeare went to school here. It was a very strict school.

This is how Shakespeare wrote his name.

Shakespeare the actor

Travelling actors visited Stratford when Shakespeare was a boy. One of the most famous actors of that time was Will Kemp. He played funny parts.

All the parts in the plays were acted by men, even the women's parts.

Shakespeare liked the plays so much he joined an acting company and travelled to London.

Shakespeare acted at a theatre called 'The Globe'.

Can you see it in the picture? It was open in the middle. The audience sat on balconies all the way round.

Globe Theatre

There were no photographs in Shakespeare's time. These are the only pictures of him we have.

Do you think they look like the same man?

Shakepeare's plays

Shakespeare's plays are performed all over the world and have been turned into operas, ballets and films.

Here are some of his most famous characters.

Hamlet

Romeo and Juliet

Bottom the weaver is in a play called 'A Midsummer Night's Dream'. He was turned into a donkey by a fairy.

Here is a carving of him on a lamp post in Stratford.

Who was Nelson?

This is Josh. He lives near a pub called The Admiral Nelson. He knows that Nelson was a famous sailor 200 years ago. Now he wants to find out more.

Has anything or anybody you know been named after Nelson?

In the Navy

Nelson came from a village in Norfolk by the sea. His mother died when he was nine.

His uncle was in the Navy. When Nelson was twelve, his uncle got him a job on a warship.

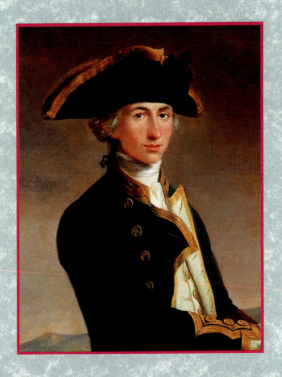

Nelson became a very good sailor. By the age of 20, he was captain of his own ship.

Here is a portrait of young Nelson that was painted at the time.

Life in the Navy was very hard 200 years ago. The food was bad and the pay was low. The ships had no engines, just lots of sails to catch the wind.

England was at war with France and Spain.

Battles at sea were very noisy and dangerous. When enemy ships met, they fired at each other with cannons.

Nelson the hero

Nelson was famous for winning sea battles. Messages were sent between his ships using flags.

Yes   No   I am on fire   Man overboard   I need help

Nelson's most famous message was:

"England expects that every man will do his duty."

Nelson went blind in one eye in a battle near Italy. Later, his arm was so badly wounded it had to be cut off.

Operations were done on board ship without any pain-killers.

Nelson's most famous battle was the Battle of Trafalgar. It was a great victory, but Nelson was hit by a bullet and died. He became a hero at home.

Nelson's ship is still moored in Portsmouth Docks. It is called 'The Victory'. Many people go to see it.

Trafalgar Square in London has a statue of Nelson on top of a tall pillar. It is called Nelson's Column.

Who was Queen Victoria?

This is Alice Victoria. Her middle name is the same as a famous Queen.

Queen Victoria lived about 100 years ago. Her time as Queen is often called the Victorian Age.

Alice has some old coins with Victoria's face on them.

One shows Victoria when she was young.

One shows Victoria when she was old.

This cup and saucer was made when Victoria had been Queen for 60 years.

Victoria was an only child. Her early years were quite lonely.

She spent her time drawing and collecting dolls.

You can see some of Victoria's dolls if you visit Kensington Palace, where she was born.

Victoria becomes Queen

Victoria's uncle was the King. When he died, he did not have any children, so Victoria became Queen. She was only eighteen. Suddenly she was famous!

Victoria was woken up and told the news.

Here is a painting of the scene.

She was crowned at Westminster Abbey.

Afterwards, she rushed home to give her dog Dash a bath. Here is a picture she drew of Dash.

Diamond Jubilee

Queen Victoria married her cousin Prince Albert. They had nine children.

Here is a photograph of them all.

Victoria was the first queen to have her photograph taken.

Queen Victoria ruled for longer than any other king or queen. When she was an old lady she had a Diamond Jubilee to mark her 60 years on the throne.

The British Empire

When Victoria was Queen, Great Britain ruled several other countries. Australia, India, Canada and parts of Africa were part of the British Empire.

Here is a photograph of two of Victoria's children wearing Indian clothes.